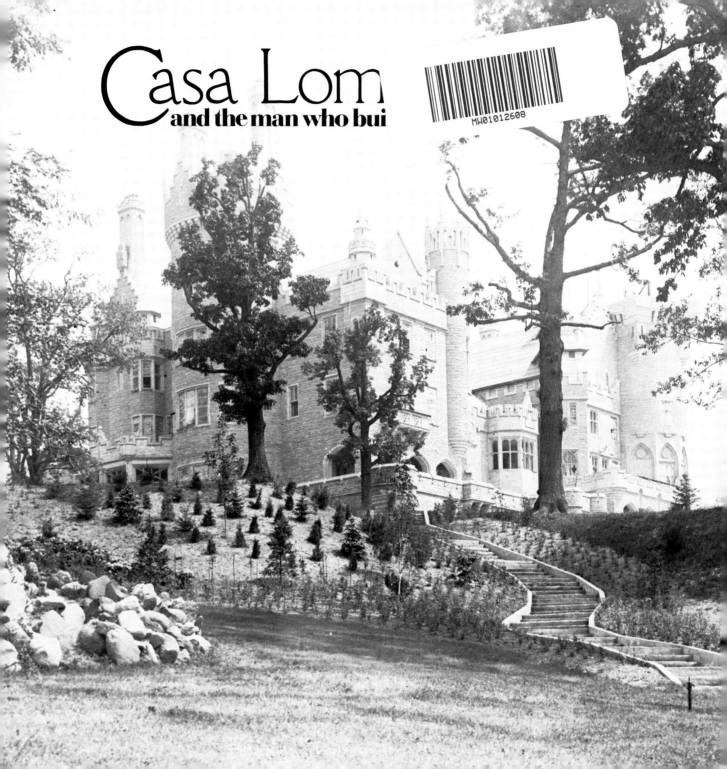

Casa Lom
and the man who bui

ON YOUR MARK...

Picture this man, Henry Pellatt, at the age of twenty. He is long and lean and wearing a runner's costume — what looks for all the world like long underwear with red shorts on top. He is doing loosening-up exercises, breathing deeply, smiling at the crowd.

GET SET...

The year is 1879, the place New York City and the occasion the North American Champion Mile Race. Henry Pellatt, the Canadian Champion, winner of last year's Dominion Mile takes his place beside the American Champion. Hundreds of onlookers tense their muscles in anticipation.

GO!

At the end of the first quarter-mile the American is an easy twenty yard leader. Pellatt seems slightly disorganized out of rhythm. Perhaps the large crowd has had its effect or the fact that the American has never been beaten has undermined Pellatt's confidence. At the half mile Pellatt seems to be almost out of contention. The few Northerners in the crowd can feel their patriotic bets melting away like spring snow. But Pellatt is no quitter and the thought of coming all this way to lose does not sit easily on one so full of pride. Henry shifts into high gear and begins to close on his opponent.

At the end of the third lap the American steals a glance over his shoulder. Pellatt is now less than ten yards behind and gaining. The American orders his legs to go faster. Still Pellatt gains — but will it be enough? The finish line in sight, Henry Pellatt explodes — he runs the last hundred yards in 12 seconds — a feat not equalled until 1930 by Jesse Owens — and wins the North American Mile in the incredible time of four minutes, thirty-two seconds, a half stride ahead of the American Champion.

Henry Mill Pellatt was born in Kingston, January 6, 1859. Two years later, his family moved to Toronto. Five more children were born and in 1866 Henry's father, Henry Sr., started the stock-broking firm of Pellatt and Osler. At 17, Henry graduated from Upper Canada College and decided it was time to see the world. This photograph was taken in a studio in Geneva, Switzerland. Henry liked many things about Europe: the art, the antiques, the military tradition, old weapons, suits of armour and the castles. How Henry loved the fairytale castles! He sketched them, memorized them, gathered in all the details and stored them away beside his other boyhood dreams. But Henry had a way of making dreams come true.

PHOTOGRAPHIE INSTANTANÉE

MÉDAILLES D'ARGENT

BOISSONNAS   GENÈVE

CALCUTTA   LYON   NEW YORK   PARIS

PEINTRE ET PHOTOGRAPHE   1870   1872   1874   1875   QUAI DE LA POSTE, 4.
EN FACE LE PONT DE LA COULOUVRENIÈRE

At the age of seventeen Henry entered his father's stockbroking business. At eighteen he joined the Queen's Own Rifles, a volunteer Toronto regiment that practised nights and weekends. At nineteen he won the Dominion Mile. At twenty-three he married Mary Dodgson, a local society girl with connections. At twenty-four, Henry Pellatt was ready to take on the world.

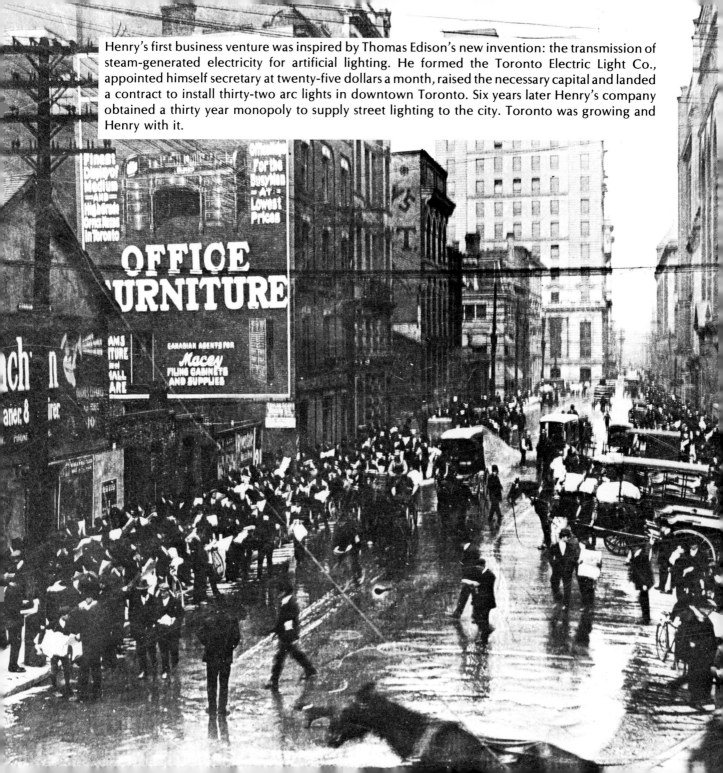

Henry's first business venture was inspired by Thomas Edison's new invention: the transmission of steam-generated electricity for artificial lighting. He formed the Toronto Electric Light Co., appointed himself secretary at twenty-five dollars a month, raised the necessary capital and landed a contract to install thirty-two arc lights in downtown Toronto. Six years later Henry's company obtained a thirty year monopoly to supply street lighting to the city. Toronto was growing and Henry with it.

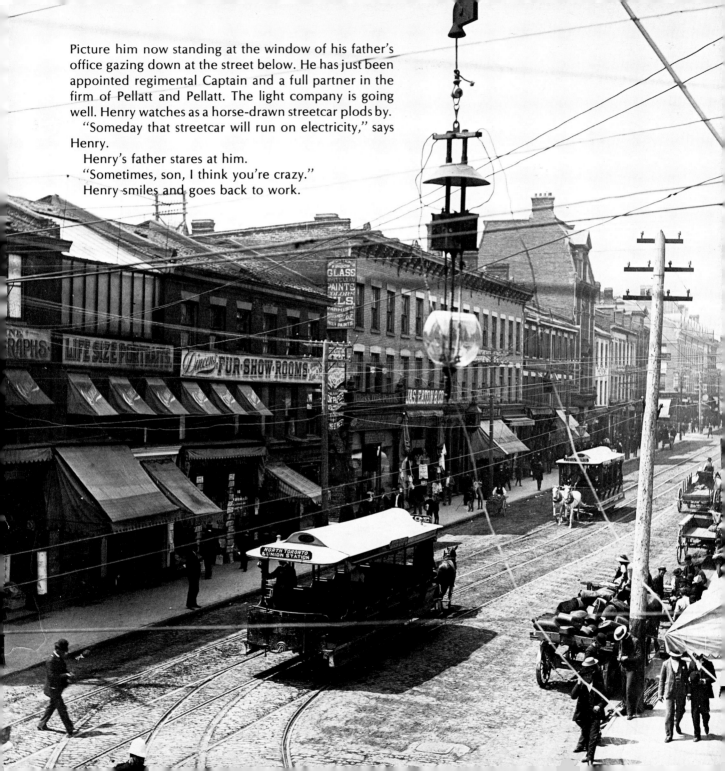

Picture him now standing at the window of his father's office gazing down at the street below. He has just been appointed regimental Captain and a full partner in the firm of Pellatt and Pellatt. The light company is going well. Henry watches as a horse-drawn streetcar plods by.

"Someday that streetcar will run on electricity," says Henry.

Henry's father stares at him.

"Sometimes, son, I think you're crazy."

Henry smiles and goes back to work.

In 1892 Henry Pellatt Sr. retired from the firm. Rumours had it Henry paid his father to retire. Henry took over and began to invest heavily in the Northwest Land Company (land for the flood of immigrants that would surely come), the Canadian Pacific Railway (which would carry the immigrants), and the Toronto Electric Railway Co. (which had a thirty year monopoly to run electric streetcars in Toronto!). To finance this frantic buying, Henry borrowed regularly from the Home Bank. In 1895 his firm owed $225,000; in 1903, $955,000. The wise old stockbrokers smirked in anticipation: "Pellatt the Plunger" was in for a great fall.

In 1897 Major Henry Pellatt went to England to celebrate Queen Victoria's Diamond Jubilee. On May 24th, the Queen's birthday, Pellatt was in charge of the honour guard at St. Paul's Cathedral — one of the highlights of his military career. Soon after our young man began to collect on his bets. Immigrants poured into Canada. The railway carried them west. Toronto expanded. More lights were needed; more streetcars; more stockbroking. On his Northwest Land Co. holdings alone, Pellatt is estimated to have made three to four million dollars! Henry had arrived.

Henry reinvested his money. In 1901 he and his friends William Mackenzie (Toronto Electric Railway), Frederik Nicholls (Canadian General Electric) and George Cox (Dominion Securities) joined together and formed Sao Paulo Tramway, Light and Power Co. in Brazil. It was so successful they incorporated the Rio de Janeiro Tramway, Light and Power Co., and in 1911 they merged the two companies to form Brascan which is today one of the biggest Canadian multi-national companies.

The four men were not done yet. With the rising cost of coal, steam-generated power was becoming expensive. In 1903, they incorporated the Electrical Development Company of Ontario and built the first Canadian generating station at Niagara Falls. Here's Henry, the president of the new company showing the site to prospective investors and later laying the cornerstone for the generating station.

In 1905, Lieutenant Colonel Pellatt was appointed aide-de-camp to Governor-General Earl Grey and later in the year was knighted by King Edward VII. *Sir* Henry Pellatt!

With his growing wealth on seemingly solid ground, Sir Henry began once more to dream of castles, but this time they were not just the vague musings of a boy but the hard plans of a man with the money to see them through. He started by buying (in his wife's name) twenty-five estate lots on the top of Davenport Hill. The property was known as Casa Loma — Spanish for "House on a hill". He bought more land in the area and in 1905 started work on the massive Casa Loma stables.

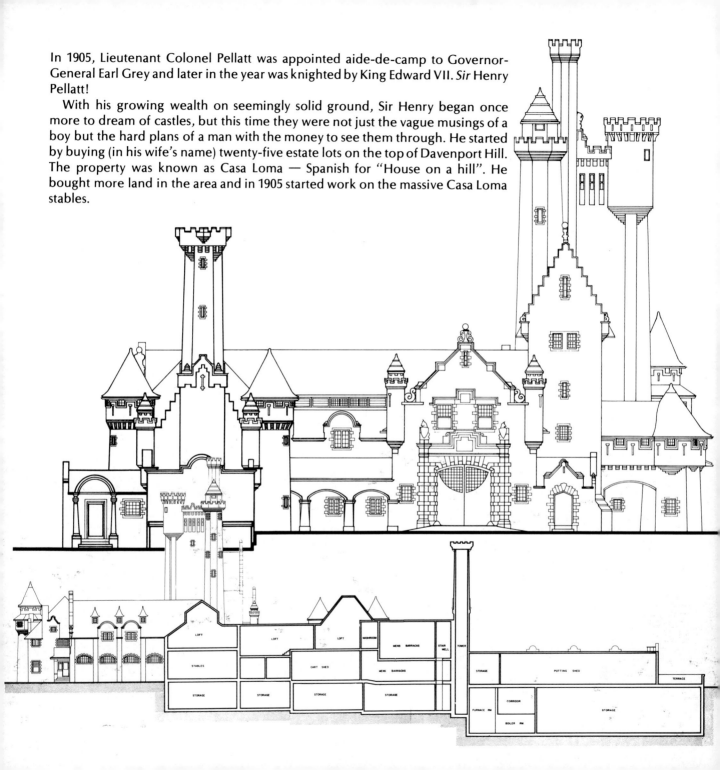

At the same time Sir Henry Pellatt built staff quarters, barracks, greenhouses, (that's Lady Pellatt wearing the pearls), a huge coal-fired heating plant for both stables and castle and a 250 metre (800') tunnel he hoped some day would connect the stables to his dream castle across the road.

Sir Henry built the stables first (cart before the horse?) as he had a multitude of valuable horses to look after and, even in those days, boarding costs were high. Secondly, he wanted to make sure there was plenty of heat ready for his future mansion. Why did he build his stables and castle with a road in between opening the whole estate to public view? Sir Henry planned to reroute the road north of the stables just as his friend Mackenzie had done with his estate. Unfortunately, between building the stables and the castle, the City of Toronto took over jurisdiction of this area from York Township and refused to let Sir Henry change the road.

The stables, made of Credit Valley stone, are reported to have cost $250,000 — no mean sum in those days. The floors were covered in Spanish tiles set in a zig-zag pattern so that the horses wouldn't slip. The stalls were made of mahogany and each horse had his name displayed in eighteen carat gold letters over his stall. The story goes that Sir Henry even had false teeth made for his favourite steed — Prince — so he could chew his oats. Across the road a huge garden and a deer park, similar to the one the King had at Windsor Castle, were constructed. Sir Henry couldn't help but smile.

A MYSTERY

SIR HENRY PELLAT:—

FREDERIC NICHOLLS:—

{ "Don't see why Adam has to go lookin' for a warmer climate. He's made this one plenty hot enough for us."

HALLOWE'EN

SIR HENRY PELLATT:—"Wouldn't it be great if you could put that bar'l on the chimbly and smoke Whitney and Beck out of house and home."

But it was not all a bed of roses. Henry was the brunt of many jokes and cartoons. The "establishment" thought him loud (so unCanadian); others pompous; still others begrudged him his success. But Henry was thick-skinned and is even said to have kept a scrapbook of all the cartoons. Yet there was one matter in which the cartoons took on a vehemence that Henry couldn't understand. The issue was the private ownership of electrical power.

A FLAW IN THE OUTLOOK

HON. ADAM BECK:—"Beautiful outlook, isn't it?"
SIR HENRY PELLATT:—"Beautiful! it would be perfect if we only had you goin' over it in a barrel."

"MORTGAGING THE HOMESTEAD."

SIR HENRY PELLATT:—"Kin nuthin' be done to prevent them sharpers, Whitney and Beck, from gettin' that poor man to put a mortgage on his home?"
MR. FREDERIC NICHOLLS:—"Nuthin' that we ain't doin kin be done!"

People began to complain of the high cost of transportation and electricity. In 1905 the Conservatives were elected in Ontario and Adam Beck, who's statue you can see on University Avenue, became a cabinet minister. In 1906, Beck set up the Hydro Electric Power Commission of Ontario and demanded the public ownership of electrical production. Pellatt and his cohorts tried to stop the movement but the tide of public opinion was against them. In 1910, Hydro opened its own plant at Niagara Falls. In 1911, Henry sold out to Mackenzie who in the end was forced to sell to the public company. For Sir Henry it was but a momentary setback — he was already on to bigger and better things.

Thanks mostly to Lieut. Col. Pellatt's effort, the Queen's Own grew into two regiments. In 1906, Sir Henry returned to New York City with nine hundred men where they put on an incredible show of military manoeuvres at Madison Square Gardens. Sir Henry wowed them and was promoted to Colonel. Then in 1910, on the fiftieth anniversary of the Queen's Own, the people of Canada were stunned with the news that Sir Henry at his own expense ($150,000) was taking 640 officers and men to England to take part in the war games. This photo shows Sir Henry with Gen. Bethune and Gen. Sir Charles Burnett at Liverpool, August 27, 1910.

On the boat going overseas the officers beat the sergeants at a tug-of-war, thanks to their anchorman — you guessed it — Sir Henry weighing in at 140 kg (300 pounds). A month was spent on manoeuvres and then the Canadians descended on London where a huge banquet was held in their honour. With war on the horizon, England was glad of this show of colonial support. Before the trip was over, Sir Henry was presented with the "Commander of Victorian Order" by King George V at Balmoral Castle. He was now *Sir Henry Pellett, C.V.O.!*

Henry was now at the peak of his career. He held twenty-one directorships in such companies as Empire Life Assurance, Canadian Steamship Lines, West Dome Mining Co., and Dofasco. He became president of the Mining Corp. of Canada. He founded the British Columbia Packers' Association. He belonged to the York Club, Albany Club, Toronto Club and the Rideau Club in Ottawa. When King George V was crowned, Sir Henry Pellatt had commemorative coins minted and distributed free to Toronto's school children. He raised money for Trinity College. He donated a surgery to Grace Hospital. He organized the St. John's Ambulance Brigade in Canada. He donated armour to the Royal Ontario Museum. Henry was a busy man. Even the depression of 1907 only slowed Sir Henry's plans momentarily. The man on the left is Mackenzie King, the future Prime Minister of Canada, who is enjoying a field day at Lake Marie (just north of Toronto) where Sir Henry has just purchased a 445 hectare (1000 acre) farm for the weekends!

Sir Henry bought the first electric car in Toronto and as the story goes drove over to the armouries to show it off to the boys. The problem was that when he got there the #★@1★# car wouldn't stop. The boys finally managed to build a wall of hay and Sir Henry gratefully rammed to a halt. I'm sure that's why he's sitting in the back. The house in the background is where Sir Henry lived while the castle was being built. It still stands just across the road from Casa Loma.

Sir Henry hired Edward Lennox, Toronto's leading architect, (he designed the "Old" City Hall). Sir Henry dumped all his sketches and ideas in Lennox's lap, saying, "Design me a castle!"

Lesser men would have quaked at the idea, but not Lennox. He promptly bought a lot near the proposed castle, and began to plan his own home — in the shadow of Casa Loma.

The plans called for 98 rooms, 3 bowling alleys, 30 bathrooms, 25 fireplaces, 5000 electric lights, an elevator, an indoor swimming pool, a 50 metre (150′) shooting gallery, a 1700 bottle temperature-controlled wine cellar, a $75,000 pipe organ and a stove big enough to cook a steer whole. The cost: $3,500,000.

The foundations are 15 metres (45') deep. The floors are 45 cm. (18") thick. Between each floor a 1.3 metre (4') crawl space makes plumbing and electrical maintenance easy. The castle had its own telephone system and one of the first built-in vacuum systems.

Henry made extensive use of steel reinforced concrete which he then faced in stone. The stones of the castle were laid by Scottish stonemasons brought over expressly for the job. When the castle was finished, these same men built the famous stone wall surrounding the castle. Cost: $250,000.

For Torontonians, the thing to do on Sunday was to walk to "The Hill" and see how Henry's Castle (or "Pellatt's Folly" as some called it) was coming along.

Peacock Alley has panelled oak walls fashioned after those in Windsor Castle. The 6 cm (2½″) thick teak flooring is held together by mahogany strips and rosewood wedges. No nails! By the way, all these interior photographs show the castle as it was in Sir Henry's day. Don't trip over the bear.

These two pictures show how Sir Henry's library looked originally. The shelves were built to hold 10,000 books. Much is made of the interesting way the wood floor in this room changes patterns depending at which end you're standing, but Sir Henry obviously preferred a good rug under his feet. The Pellatt coat of arms — "Devant Si Je Puis" (Foremost If I Can) — is repeated on the plaster ceiling. The wall at the end is now gone. The doorway led to the dining room. Notice the carved wooden chairs in the right hand photograph. I'd like six please and I need them by Friday.

This is the dining room. There's a story that one day two workmen were trying to hang a huge chandelier in the castle when they dropped it. Just as it hit the floor exploding into a thousand little pieces, Lady Pellatt walked into the room.

"Don't worry. We'll just order another one."

Of course, with such a great house, the Pellatts were always entertaining. Dinner was a favourite time for guests and Sir Henry, not wishing to appear boorish, ate moderately. After dinner he would excuse himself, stroll into the kitchen and wolf down the other meal the cook had waiting for him.

The bronze doors ($10,000 each) on the right lead to the conservatory.

Here is the conservatory before all the plants arrived. It's obviously tea and tour time. One day Lady Eaton, who lived close by, was escorted through the castle by Sir Henry. He showed her where the grand staircase linking the main hall to the second floor was to go. (Unfortunately it was being made in Europe and with the outbreak of W.W.I. its arrival was delayed indefinitely.) "You know," said Sir Henry, "I wish I had another million dollars. Do you know what I'd do? I'd finish this house and then I'd die happy."

It doesn't take much imagination to see the riot of colour in this photo. Sir Henry had steam pipes run through the dirt in the planters so he could grow all kinds of exotic plants. Directly overhead you can catch a glimpse of the $12,000 stained glass dome. The swimming pool is under this room in the basement.

Still on the first floor, let's take a stroll into Henry's mahogany panelled study, the smallest room in the castle. Here is the replica of Napoleon's desk. To the right of the fireplace is the secret passageway leading to the basement vault and to the left the hidden staircase to the second floor. All we need is some buried treasure and a ghost!

This is Sir Henry's bedroom complete with a secret pillar for important papers...

...and his marble bathroom with the Rube Goldberg plumbing. The strange object on the left is a footbath. The shelf above it was for a telephone but in this photo Sir Henry must have been talking to his cologne.

This is Lady Pellatt's bedroom in 1917. She was a semi-invalid when she lived in Casa Loma and spent most of her time here in her gigantic suite.

There was always something happening at the castle. Sir Henry would have the regiment up for a weekend or Lady Pellatt would entertain the local Girl Guide troops.

How about having Canon Cody over for a costume tea party?

Ethnic folk dancing?

Casa Loma became the social showcase of the city. In 1921 Sir Henry was promoted to Major General and Lady Pellatt received the Silver Fish Award for her life-long devotion to the Girl Guide movement.

But storm clouds were brewing and Henry's firm was heavily in debt to the Home Bank. His money was tied up in real estate developments not the least of which was the prestigious subdivision he envisioned for the land around the castle; but because of the war and the depression that followed it people were not buying. Henry's debts grew.

The cost of maintaining Casa Loma skyrocketed. Fuel costs soared. Taxes rose to $1000 a month. The forty servants had to be paid. Henry, growing older and more complacent, had lost his money magic. On August 17, 1923 the Home Bank went bankrupt. Pellatt and Pellatt owed $1,700,000. Much of the testimony in April and May 1924, concerning the demise of the Home Bank, centred around Sir Henry. It was all too much for Lady Pellatt who died in April of a heart-attack. Sir Henry had had enough.

Persian Rugs Knocked Down for Price of Good Doormats

Plenty of Spectators, but Few Bidders, when Casa Loma Treasures Go Under Auctioneer's Hammer — Ale Glasses Sell for $26 a Dozen in "Dry" Ontario — Grandfather's Clock Goes for $155 and Sir Henry's Bath Scales for $10.

Treasures from the ends of the earth, gathered after a ceaseless hunt and a great deal of trouble in some cases, were disposed of in quick succession yesterday when the contents of Casa Loma, the handsome residence of Sir Henry Pellatt, were sold at auction.

A fairly large crowd — most of whom, were purchasers — gathered in the conservatory where C.H. Henderson, the auctioneer, disposed of the contents of some of the china cupboards, the sitting rooms, equipment and furniture from the serveries and pantries, and the garden statuary.

Garden Vases at $16 Each.

A carved marble fountain with a child's figure supporting a dolphin, of exquisite design and workmanship, brought only $200. The same fortunate buyer secured five large garden vases at $16 each. Another active purchaser, from Detroit, for $25 got two handsome brass sundials.

Of carved marble was a conservatory bench which brought only feeble response and was finally disposed of for $45. Worth $1,000 was a buffalo head that the auctioneer regretfully knocked down for $50 after coaxing along the bidding.

Rare Old China Sacrificed.

Rare old china of the eggshell variety and also of the thicker quality which was found in great great-grandmother's wedding set was offered.

Sacrifice and slaughter are the only words that truly describe the sale of the china. By paying only $43 the Detroit buyer carried off 19 pieces of a rare old Dresden china dinner set, one piece of which is really worth the total price. Twenty-two pieces of old Staffordshire Copper Lustre on blue, decorated in panels, brought only $55. An old Spode platter with landscape in blue and white was knocked down for $22, while an early Spode tea set in blue and white, decorated in Oriental figures — 23 pieces — received as the highest bid just $57.

There was some lively bidding on Georgian mahogany dining furniture.

Two ladies, one from Montreal and the other from Detroit, carried off many of the treasures.

An Etching for $10.

"Oh, mother, you had better buy that," urged a son when Mr. Henderson presented a handsome proof etching, "Moorland and Mist," by Peter Graham, R.A. The mother had been bidding feverishly on a lot of china and crystal that was of no interest whatever to the boy, but he did fancy the etching. His mother feebly murmured something that sounded like "$2", but a more daring bidder said "$10," and away went the treasure.

"Moonlight," an oil on canvas by Homer Watson, went for $55; "Coming Storm," by W. Hancock, went as high as $82, while Cresswell's "Landscape" and Dawson's "Portsmouth Habor" brought only $25 apiece.

"A Persian rug for the price of a doormat," muttered the auctioneer as rug after rug was knocked down at a 'slaughter' price. Karacs and Daghistans for $40, $45 and $50, of good size and exquisite design and coloring were quickly sold. A Royal Hermaushah worth $4,000 sold for $825.

A Kazac, a very old collectors piece, was purchased for $54 for Sir William Mulock. There were several Lilihans and Shirvans, but $62 was the highest offer for any of them.

Curious Ale Glasses.

"Ale — out of those things!" was a remark overhead in the audience when a tray of tall, slender, flaring glasses was put on the table. These were listed as old English ale glasses and sold at $26 for the dozen.

Bolts of fine silk brocade and printed linen were sold in the piece at extremely low prices. Chesterfields and arm chairs brought $40 and $20, respectively. A grandfather's clock in Chippendale mahogany case, with a brass and silver engraved dial, brought only a very low price.

CASA LOMA'S ART TREASURES SCATTERED TO THE FOUR WINDS UNDER AUCTIONEER'S HAMMER.

Wonderful Dinner Services, Antiques, Exquisite Cut Glasses, Historic Relics of Kings and Valuable Paintings Bought by Bidders from Every Point of Compass.

Casa Loma's great rooms and hallways are being rapidly and systematically stripped of their treasures. Yesterday's crowd of purchasers doubled that of Monday's and prices were decidedly higher. Auctioneer Henderson many, many times had to raise his voice and demand silence of the enthusiastic gathering as the outstanding pieces were put up for sale.

Some Fevered Bidding.

Gordon Edwards, a nephew of Senator Edwards of Ottawa, carried off many of the handsomest and most valuable offerings of the day. The M. Imple de Sevres dinner service of 132 pieces, Royal blue and gold, with painted miniatures of Napoleon and his officers and Court beauties, Mr. Edwards got for $2,600. The first bid was $1,000, then it crept up by hundreds, Mrs. Asher Pearce of Montreal running him a close race. This set is one of three, being a special commission by Napoleon and presented to Marshal le Fleurve. It is valued at 80,000 francs.

"What is the meaning of this?" demanded Mr. Henderson furiously when some cautious bidder suggested $1,000 as a start on the massive solid silver dinner service originally the property of Comte de Garbier. The bidding went up to $2,000; then this set also went to Mr. Edwards. In the morning he purchased a Louis XVI solid silver flower basket for $165, a pair of Louis XVI solid silver flower baskets for $150 each, two Sheffield octagonal flower tubes at $40 each, and four smaller tubes to match at $27.50 each.

Sir Henry vacated the castle taking three vans of personal belongings with him. The rest he put up for auction. Collectors came from all over North America to bid for Casa Loma's treasures during the five day sale. The $1,500,000 collection disappeared for $250,000. A solid bronze buffalo head sold for $50. (The unfortunate buyer couldn't lift his purchase and was forced to sell it to a man with eight strong friends.) The $75,000 organ, which the 76 year-old auctioneer played, much to the delight of the packed crowd, sold for $40. Sir Henry told one reporter: "It is a sale which breaks my heart"; but later as he wandered through the castle, chatting and joking with old friends, he added: "The process is something like getting a tooth pulled — once over, one proceeds to forget all about it".

SENATOR HARDY PAYS $10,000 FOR EIGHT PELLATT CURTAINS.

Ontario's Millionaires Bid for Masterpieces Stripped from Casa Loma's Art Gallery — Paul Peel's "The Shepherdess" Brings $4,100.

Fine masterpieces stripped from the wall of Sir Henry Pellatt's art gallery for the fourth day's sale at Casa Loma for the most part, will remain in Canada. Early yesterday afternoon the pictures were brought out, and the large crowd in the conservatory grew tense with excitement. A disturbance was caused at the entrances by people interested particularly in these offerings, who were unable to crowd into the room.

"You ladies are not interested in pictures," said T. Jenkins, as he endeavoured to persuade a group of spectators to depart and make room for the real buyers. There was a stir, and a number, frankly admitting disinterest, vacated their seats.

Paul Peel's "The Shepherdess", one of his last and most important paintings, brought an initial bid of $1,000. After jumping quickly by thousands it was finally bought by J.P. Bickell for $4,100. Mr. Bickell also got the Van Dyck, "Robert Devereaux" for $3,500. The valuable Reynolds, "Horace Walpole" also went to Mr. Bickell for $2,700.

$5,100 for Watercolor.

Gordon Edwards, Ottawa, gave $5,100 for the Turner watercolor, "View of Fonthill Abbey", paying the biggest price of the day for pictures. The bidding was keen, but Mr. Edwards was prepared to top the list.

Seymour H. Knox, Buffalo, prominent purchaser during the last three days of the sale, gave $2,150 for the oil on canvas, "J. Singleton Copley, R.A." from Lord Lyndhurst's collection, by George Romney, R.A.

"On the St. Lawrence," by Paul Peel, went to T. Jenkins for $400. Mrs. A. Pierce, Montreal, gave $625 for the Wilkie "Portrait of Himself," painted for Sir Robert Peel. Charles S. Hirach, New York, got a Krossman, "Winter Landscape, Holland" for $145, and W.E. Atkinson's "Dutch Canal" at $42.50.

"The new frame cost $27, and then you talk of $85 for a Monticelli," snorted T. Jenkins to Auctioneer Henderson as he called for offers on the "Harbor Showing Cottage". Merritt Malloney got it for $125. The same buyer gave $400 for the "Portrait of a Lady," by Sir Thomas Lawrence P.R.A. and $500 for an Emile Jacque "Landscape With Sheep."

Senator A.C. Hardy of Brockville was a frequent purchaser during the sale along with Mr. Segsworth, Grace Scott, J. Pearson, L.O. Lumbers, H.H. Drummond, W.T. Harris, J.C. Hamilton (Listowel), F.W. Cowan (Oshawa), H.J. Alexander, A. Donald, Mrs. Owen, Mrs. G.S. Black (Montreal), J. Crane, William Moore (Barrie), M.I. Jackson (Seaforth), O.B. Jones, R.W. Leonard (St. Catharines), William Croft, B.F. Duncan and Roberts' Art Gallery.

"Who ever heard of a Constable being sold for $600," growled Mr. Jenkins, when the bidding lagged at the figure on the "At Langham, Suffolk". John A. Pearson finally gave $875 for it.

$10,000 for Curtains.

Senator Hardy gave $10,000 for eight curtains in D'Aubusson tapestries in unique coloring and texture. The first offer was $5,000 leaping immediately from that to eight, then to nine thousand, with the final bid of ten thousand from the Senator.

"Don't take less than a $5 bid", admonished Mr. Jenkins to Auctioneer Henderson.

"Take anything", promptly responded Mr. Henderson, as he exhibited a pair of Sevres vases in royal blue and gold, whose companion pair repose in the Muses du Louvre. Mrs. A.J. Freeman of Ottawa got them for $725 each.

Sensational sales of the day occurred when the magnificent gold drawing-room suites, handsomely carved and upholstered in Louis XVI, d'Aubusson tapestry, were produced. There were two of these suites from the stately Napoleon drawing-room. The name of Mrs. Freeman of Ottawa was heard when the large sofa of the first suite was knocked down to her for $550. Despite the numerous contestants for these pieces, Mrs. Freeman carried off the six elbow chairs at $225 each, a $240 window seat and a large threefold fire screen for $200.

CASA LOMA'S STORE

Auctioneers Find It Impossible to Sell All Articles on Time

SOME LIVELY INCIDENTS

Five days of the stupendous auction sale are over and still Casa Loma is not entirely divested of its furnishings. At the close of yesterday's offering, which should have concluded the sale, Thomas Jenkins announced that, as this was an impossibility, the remaining articles would be sold on a later day, the date of which will be announced shortly. This will include the contents of the maids' rooms and the odds and ends gathered up at the last minute from the many cupboards and crannies in the castle.

Gordon Edwards, Ottawa, made another interesting purchase yesterday morning when he gave $1,150 for a magnificent Louis XVI 30-day grandfather clock with a finely modelled bronze figure surmounting it. Another Louis XVI time-piece, an ormolu mantel clock bearing the figures of "Day" and "Night" went as a real bargain for George Macdougall for $200. The same buyer gave $320 for a pair of Louis XVI mahogany pedestals supporting bronze figures with Girandole, six lights, in ormolu.

William McMullen, Montreal, got a set of ten Jacobean oak hall chairs at $32.50 each. R.S. Campbell gave $90 for a Jacobean oak hall seat.

Casa Loma's complete laundry was purchased by Langley's "My Valet" for $1,125. The immaculate kitchen equipment will be separated, Gordon Edwards got two large refrigerators and a Jewel gas range with grill for $300. Langley's paid $675 for the remainder, which consisted of a steam table, hot plate cabinet, carrying table and a hot-plate cupboard.

Mrs. T. Crawford Brown, got Sir Henry Pellatt's magnificent Louis XVI bedstead with box springs and hair mattress for $380. A mahogany dressing table went to Mrs. A. Sankey for $47.50 while R.S. McLaughlin paid $250 for the Louis XVI rosewood desk richly embellished in gilt ormolu.

From this same bedroom of Sir Henry's, Gordon Edwards got a chest of drawers for $75; Merritt Mahoney, a mahogany chest of drawers with covered spiral columns $300, and J. Henry Peters a wrought-iron fender with fire basket and set of fire implements for $100.

"My that is a beauty and a real bargain!" was a remark heard when different pieces were put up for bid.

"Damaged and repaired" explained Mr. Jenkins when auctioneer Henderson called for bidding on two antique chairs. Despite this injunction the gentleman who paid $25 apiece for them was back in about a quarter of an hour with the mended chair and grievous complaints.

Amid much laughter the despised article was resold to another buyer for $17.50.

As a scarlet banner waving gallantly across the front of the room, numerous yards of stair carpet was exhibited to the excited audience. Sevres vases, Empire drawing-room suites and billiard tables can only be used in a mansion, but any home at some time or other has need of a stair carpet. It brought $30. Another roll brought $60. W.A. Curtis paid $17.50 for a brass bedstead.

Only $70 was the price given by W.W. Snider for an early Italian carved arm chair covered in green cut velvet. R.W. Taylor with a bid of $105, got a massive walnut hall seat with full pier mirror, elaborately carved and brass mounted.

Miss Helen Gibbons, London, for $25 got an oil print, "Miss Farren" by Sir Thomas Lawrence, and the "Boy in Red" by the same artist went to Norman McEachren for $40. W. Murphy's "India Orchestra" brought $42.50 from P.J. White. W. Bloor gave $72.50 for an oil on canvas "Rapids on the Wangnie River" by Val de Lawron. "Wakataki" by the same artist, brought a bid of $75 from P.J. White.

"Auld Lang Syne" played on the Karn organ by no less a personage than Auctioneer Henderson himself, brought from the audience round after round of applause, but only feeble bidding. Despite the delightful demonstration of the instrument H. Franklin got it for $40.

Exquisite furniture and hangings from the bedrooms and dressing rooms excited much envy in the hearts of a large number of the women in the audience, which was practically as large as on the biggest days of the sale.

William Moore of Barrie got several articles from the Wedgwood blue and white bedroom.

So Sir Henry Pellatt and his dream castle went their separate ways. In January 1926, a huge party was held at Sir Henry's King Township estate to celebrate his fifty years with the Queen's Own. The regiment was commanded by Colonel Reg Pellatt, D.S.O., Sir Henry's son. In 1927, Henry married Catherine Merritt of St. Catharines. Just before Christmas, 1929, the second Lady Pellatt died of cancer. The great Depression forced the sale of the King Estate (now the Marylake Monastery) and Sir Henry's Rosedale home (78 Crescent Road). Henry moved to a small house and with his remaining money helped his son Reg in the stockbroking business.

Over the years there have been many plans for Casa Loma. It was to be a home for war veterans. Hollywood star Mary Pickford (born in Toronto) tried to use it in the movies. A high school, a convent and an Orange lodge were the next proposals. When this photo was taken the castle was being run as an exclusive hotel. Lady Pellatt's suite became a billiard room. Hard times ended that quarter of a million dollar dream.

Finally in 1936, after years of neglect, the Kiwanis Club of West Toronto leased Casa Loma from the city as a tourist attraction.

Casa Loma is now visited by more than 450,000 people annually. It's a favourite place for dances, weddings, receptions and school tours. The profits from these events are used by the Kiwanis Club for charitable work throughout the community.

In 1937, the Kiwanis Club invited Sir Henry back to Casa Loma as a guest speaker. As he rose to speak, Sir Henry's eyes filled with tears.

"I built Casa Loma principally as a place where people would enjoy themselves. Your club is now using it for that purpose and bringing enjoyment and happiness to countless people. It could not be put to a better use. I am satisfied."

In January 1939, the Queen's Own Rifles threw an eightieth birthday party for their grand old man at the Royal York Hotel. The band played, the men sang, Queen Mary sent a telegram of congratulations. This was Henry's last hurrah. On March 8, Sir Henry Pellatt died.

Sir Henry's funeral was the largest in Toronto's history. Thousands lined King Street to catch a glimpse of the horse-drawn gun carriage bearing the casket. Sir Henry's Major General hat and presentation sword rode atop the Union Jack. Soldiers, bundled up against the cold, marched to the sombre beat of muffled drums. The Regimental Sergeant-Major followed on foot carrying Sir Henry's decorations on a purple pillow. Behind him a riderless stallion shuddered in the chill air. The Band of the Queen's Own Rifles played a funeral dirge.

Sir Henry would have been proud.

ISBN 0-919822-48-7

© John Denison, 1982

Published by
Stoddart Publishing Co. Limited
34 Lesmill Road
Toronto, Canada
M3B 2T6
(416) 445-3333

A BOSTON MILLS PRESS BOOK
Erin, Ontario   N0B 1T0

Printed at Ampersand, Guelph, Ontario

Photo Credits:
City of Toronto Archives, 2, 7, 8, 13, 14, 15, 20, 21, 24-41, 44-47
City of Toronto Property Dept., 5, 12, 22
Ontario Hydro Archives, 10, 11, 16, 17
Public Archives of Canada, 1, 48
Queen's Own Rifles of Canada, Regimental Museum, Calgary, Alberta, 18, 19
Ontario Archives, 4
Nottman Photographic Archives, 6